G. Schirmer's Editions
of
Oratorios and Cantatas

THE MESSIAH
An Oratorio

For Four-Part Chorus of Mixed Voices,
Soprano, Alto, Tenor, and Bass Soli
and Piano

by

G. F. HANDEL

Edited by
T. TERTIUS NOBLE

Revised According to
Handel's Original Score by
MAX SPICKER

The Choruses (with Piano Acc.)

Ed. 1500

G. SCHIRMER, Inc.

DISTRIBUTED BY

HAL•LEONARD®
CORPORATION
7777 W. BLUEMOUND RD. P.O. BOX 13819 MILWAUKEE, WI 53213

CONTENTS

THE MESSIAH

PART I

G. F. Händel

Isaiah xl: 5

35131

*) According to the original score.

No. 5. RECITATIVE FOR BASS—"Thus Saith the Lord"
No. 6. AIR FOR BASS—"But Who May Abide the Day of His Coming?"
No. 7. CHORUS—"And He Shall Purify"

Malachi iii: 8

Allegro

un - - to the Lord an of - fer - ing in right - eous -

un - - to the Lord an of - fer - ing in right - - eous -

un - - to the Lord an of - fer - ing in right - - eous -

un - - to the Lord an of - fer - ing in right - - eous -

ness, in right - eous - ness.

ness, in right-eous - ness.

ness, in right-eous - ness.

ness, in right - eous - ness.

mf

No. 8. RECITATIVE FOR ALTO—"Behold! A Virgin Shall Conceive"
No. 9. AIR FOR ALTO, AND CHORUS—"O Thou That Tellest Good Tidings to Zion"

No. 10.   RECITATIVE FOR BASS—"For Behold, Darkness Shall Cover the Earth"

No. 11.   AIR FOR BASS—"The People That Walked in Darkness"

No. 12.   CHORUS—"For Unto Us a Child is Born"

Isaiah ix: 6

No. 13.   PASTORAL SYMPHONY
No. 14.   RECITATIVE FOR SOPRANO—"There Were Shepherds Abiding in the Field"
            RECITATIVE FOR SOPRANO—"And Lo! The Angel of the Lord Came Upon
                Them"
No. 15.   RECITATIVE FOR SOPRANO—"And the Angel Said Unto Them"
No. 16.   RECITATIVE FOR SOPRANO—"And Suddenly There Was With the Angel"

No. 17.   CHORUS—"Glory to God"

Luke ij· **14**

40

*) Original score has in bass here:

PART II

No. 22. CHORUS—"Behold the Lamb of God"

No. 23. AIR FOR ALTO—"He Was Despised"
No. 24. CHORUS—"Surely He Hath Borne Our Griefs"

No. 25. CHORUS—"And With His Stripes We Are Healed"

Isaiah liii: 5

No. 26. CHORUS "All We Like Sheep Have Gone Astray"

Isaiah liii: **6**

No. 27. RECITATIVE FOR TENOR—"All They That See Him, Laugh Him to Scorn"

No. 28. CHORUS—"He Trusted in God That He Would Deliver Him"

Psalm xxii: 8

No. 29. RECITATIVE FOR TENOR—"Thy Rebuke Hath Broken His Heart"

No. 30. AIR FOR TENOR—"Behold, And See If There Be Any Sorrow"

No. 31. RECITATIVE FOR TENOR—"He Was Cut Off Out of the Land of the Living"

No. 32. AIR FOR TENOR—"But Thou Didst Not Leave His Soul in Hell"

No. 33. CHORUS—"Lift Up Your Heads, O Ye Gates"

*) Händel's score has here, and in all similar cases, "this" King, not "the" King. It has become tradi-
tional, however, to sing "the" King.

*No. 34. RECITATIVE FOR TENOR—"Unto Which of the Angels Said He"

*No. 35. CHORUS—"Let All the Angels of God Worship Him"

*) Generally omitted

*No. 36.   AIR FOR BASS—"Thou Art Gone Up On High"
No. 37.   CHORUS—"The Lord Gave the Word"

Psalm lxviii: **11**

-pa-ny of the preach - ers,

-pa-ny, the com-pa-ny of the preach - ers,

com - - - - -pa-ny of the preach - ers,

-pa-ny of the preach - ers,

A

great was the com - pa-ny of the preachers. The Lord gave the word:

great was the com-pa-ny of the preachers. The Lord gave the word;

great was the com-pa-ny of the preachers.

great was the com - pa-ny of the preachers.

A

great was the com - - - - -pa-ny, the com - - -

great was the com - - - - -pa-ny, the com - - -

Great was the com - pa-ny, the com - - - - -pa-ny, the

Great was the com - pa-ny, the com - - - - -pa-ny, the

Ped.

No. 38.   AIR FOR SOPRANO—"How Beautiful Are the Feet of Them"
No. 39.   CHORUS—"Their Sound is Gone Out Into All Lands"
Romans x:18

No. 40. AIR FOR BASS—"Why do the Nations so Furiously Rage Together?"

No. 41. CHORUS—"Let Us Break Their Bonds Asunder"

Psalm ii: 3

No. 42.   RECITATIVE FOR TENOR—"He That Dwelleth in Heaven"
No. 43.   AIR FOR TENOR—"Thou Shalt Break Them"
No. 44.   CHORUS—"Hallelujah!"

Rev. xix: **6**; xi: **15**; xix: **16**

108

* Händel's score has here **)

END OF PART II

PART III

No. 45. AIR FOR SOPRANO—"I Know That My Redeemer Liveth"
No. 46. CHORUS—"Since by Man Came Death"

1 Cor. xv: 21

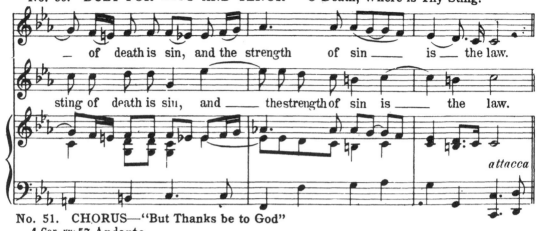

No. 51.   CHORUS—"But Thanks be to God"

1 Cor. xv: 57   Andante

No. 52. AIR FOR SOPRANO—"If God be for Us, Who can be Against Us?"

No. 53. CHORUS—"Worthy is the Lamb That Was Slain"

Rev. v: **12, 13**

*) See foot-note on page 196.